WHAT
LIVING
THINGS
EAT

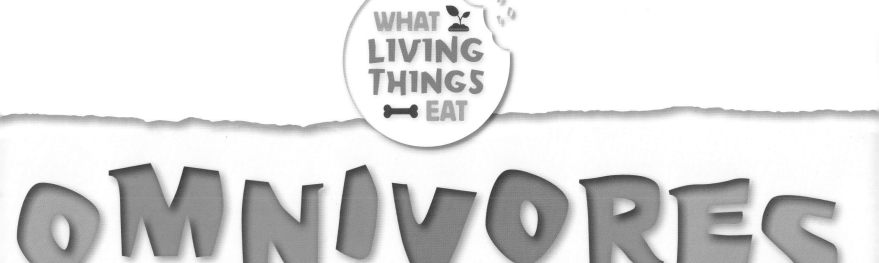

OMNIVORES

By Harriet Brundle

BookLife
PUBLISHING

©2019
BookLife Publishing
King's Lynn
Norfolk PE30 4LS

A catalogue record for this book is available from the British Library.

ISBN: 978-1-78637-466-0

Written by:
Harriet Brundle

Edited by:
Holly Duhig

Designed by:
Jasmine Pointer

Photocredits:

Images are courtesy of Shutterstock.com. With thanks to Getty Images, Thinkstock Photo and iStockphoto.

Front cover – Eric Isselee, LittlePerfectStock, mariait, DioGen, Smit, Nosyrevy, Jim Cumming, Imageman, schankz, Leo Blanchette. 2 – Michele Aldegh. 4 – Volodymyr Burdiak. 5 – Peter Gudella. 6 – Danita Delmont. 7 – BGSmith. 8 – Igorsky. 9 – OCS. 10 – Menno Schaefer. 11 – colin robert varndel, DejaVuDesigns. 12 – MartinRed. 13 – Smit. 14 – Billion Photos. 15 – AG-PHOTOS. 16 – Dudarev Mikhail. 17 – Ortis, ajt, photolinc, Eric Isselee, Luca Santilli, Krasowit, 3DMI, Kovaleva_Ka, stockphoto mania, janaph, Veniamin Kraskov, Drakuliren, volkova Natalia, Lana Langlois. 18 – stockphoto mania. 19 – Sergey Furtaev. 20 – Phil Stev. 21 – Dr Morley Read. 22 – Buffy1982. 23 – Dennis Jacobsen, Fremme.

CONTENTS

Words that look like <u>this</u> can be found in the glossary on page 24.

ALL ABOUT FOOD

Animals need food, water, air and shelter in order to stay alive. Food is very important because it is full of <u>nutrients</u> that provide the energy animals need to move and grow.

Animals also need energy to do important jobs such as breathing and <u>digesting</u> their food.

This spider is waiting for its dinner to land on its web.

You are a living thing and so you need food to survive too. Food for animals comes in lots of different shapes and sizes. You might enjoy a bowl of pasta for your dinner while a spider might prefer a fly or two for theirs!

WHAT IS AN OMNIVORE?

An omnivore is an animal that eats a range of different foods, including both meat and plant matter. For example, a skunk will eat grasses or nuts but may also enjoy eating a <u>rodent</u> or lizard.

Lots of different types of animals are omnivores, including some fish and insects.

This bear is feeding on berries.

Finding food can be easier for omnivores because they have more choice. Carnivores, which are animals that only eat meat, must find and catch their food whereas omnivores can eat whatever food is most easily available.

PREDATORS

Predators are animals that find, catch and kill other animals for their food. Although omnivores do not rely on the animals they catch to survive, meat makes up an important part of their diet.

Some birds are omnivores. This American robin will eat both worms and berries.

Animals have changed over time to make it easier to catch their food. This is called adaptation.

Some animals have adapted so that they can outrun their prey, while others use <u>camouflage</u>. Omnivores have adapted as well. Raccoons use their long fingers to reach plants.

PREY

Prey is any animal that is hunted and caught by a predator. Omnivores can often be both predator and prey. A fox is a predator when it catches a rabbit but prey when it is caught by a wolf.

Cubs are more <u>vulnerable</u> to predators.

Some badgers have loose skin so if they are caught by another animal, they can turn and bite back!

Animals that are prey have also adapted to make it harder to be caught by a predator. Some animals use spikes, spines or stings for protection. Lobsters use their large claws to defend themselves.

SCAVENGERS

Some omnivores will eat the meat and bones of an animal that has died <u>naturally</u> or has been left behind after other predators have eaten from it. These animals are known as scavengers. Some omnivorous scavengers will feed on rotting plants too.

A range of different animals can be scavengers, including birds and insects.

In some countries humans eat cockroaches.

Cockroaches are omnivores that will scavenge on any food that is available to them. Cockroaches will eat almost anything they come across. They are able to survive in a range of different <u>habitats</u> all around the world.

THE FOOD CHAIN

A food chain shows how all the different animals rely on each other for food. A food chain usually starts with a producer and animals further up the food chain are known as consumers.

A producer is something which makes its own food, such as a plant.

Most **species** could become **overpopulated** if their predator is no longer there.

Food chains are important because they keep our **ecosystems** balanced. If you were to remove an omnivore from a food chain, it could cause an overpopulation of the animals or plants that they usually eat.

Lots of food chains that link together are known as a food web.

As well as producers and omnivores, food chains usually include <u>herbivores</u> and carnivores. Each of the arrows in a food chain shows the direction the energy is moving in.

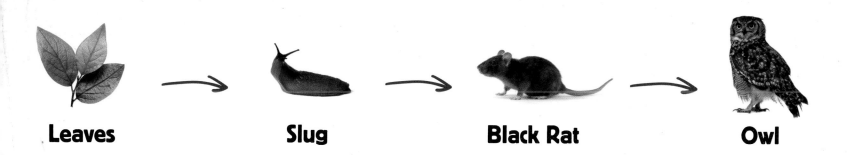

Leaves → **Slug** → **Black Rat** → **Owl**

Seaweed → **Lobster** → **Cod** → **Shark**

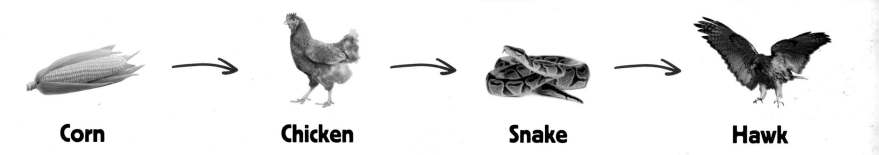

Corn → **Chicken** → **Snake** → **Hawk**

Leaves → **Giraffe** → **Lion**

Omnivores can appear at different stages of a food chain. A bear might appear higher up a food chain than a rat, but they are both omnivores.

Grass → **Moose** → **Brown Bear**

TEETH

Most omnivores have a combination of teeth which help them to eat the different types of food in their diet. Omnivores often have sharp front <u>incisors</u> and <u>canines</u>, which they use to rip and tear the meat they eat.

Chickens are omnivores but they have no teeth at all. They swallow their food whole!

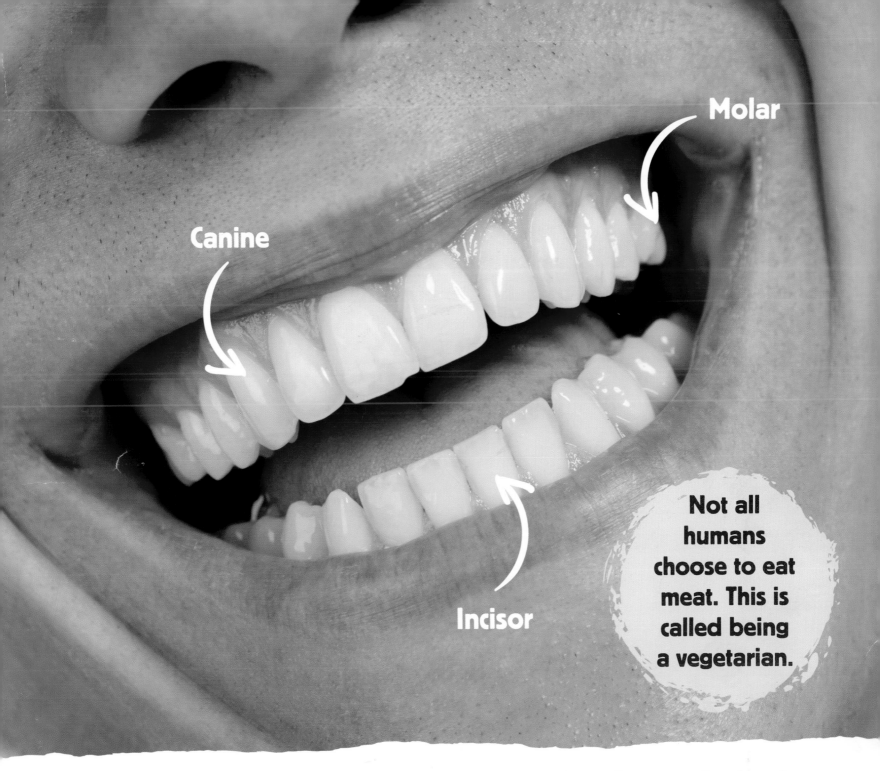

Molar

Canine

Incisor

Not all humans choose to eat meat. This is called being a vegetarian.

Omnivores usually have large, flat teeth called molars at the back of their mouths. These are used for grinding up the plants they eat. Humans are omnivores. We have sharp teeth at the front of our mouths and molars at the back of our mouths.

DIGESTION

Different types of animals have digestive systems which are better suited to dealing with the types of food they eat. Omnivores usually have digestive systems which can process both meat and plants.

A monkey's digestive system can process fruits, nuts and insects!

A varied diet means that omnivores are more likely to survive changes to their habitat.

Omnivores eat a range of different foods. If they eat something their **digestive systems** cannot process, the food will go through their body and come out as poo.

One of the smallest omnivores is the ant. Most ants feast on a wide range of foods including other insects.

Pigs are omnivores. Pigs aren't fussy about what they eat; in fact, they'll usually eat anything they can get hold of!

Lots of different species of monkey are omnivores. The pygmy marmoset is one of the smallest species of monkey and only weighs around 110 grams.

Pygmy
Marmoset

Did you know that ground squirrels are omnivores too?
They eat nuts and plants but will also eat insects.

GLOSSARY

camouflage	a way of hiding
canines	pointed teeth
digesting	the process of food being broken down in the body
ecosystems	all the plants and animals which live in a particular area
habitats	the homes of animals, plants or other organisms
herbivores	an animal that only eats plant matter
incisors	sharp teeth at the front of the mouth
naturally	as a result of nature
nutrients	needed for life and growth
overpopulated	too many of a living thing in one place
rodent	animals such as rats, mice and hamsters
species	a group of similar individuals who can breed
vulnerable	able to be attacked

INDEX